*A PROPRIETARY TECHNIQUE OF SACHIN BHATIA

BREAKER CANDLE TECHNIQUE

YOUR FIRST STEP TOWARDS FINANCIAL NIRVANA

SACHIN BHATIA &
RAMESH PATRA

INDIA • SINGAPORE • MALAYSIA

ISBN 979-8-89067-752-5

Education is just opening the door, work ethic and application is the rest.

– Ramesh Patra

CONTENTS

PREFACE

If you have a trading method but you can't stick to it, or you are struggling to be profitable, or your psychology seems to be getting in the way of your trading success (like over-thinking or making incorrect decisions), this book can give you some insights and tips to overcome these challenges. Also, Sachin Bhatia's *Breaker Candle Technique* discussed in this book, can help you completely change your trading strategies, which will eventually help you make money consistently.

The *Breaker Candle Technique* will help you get a better and clearer picture of the market, enabling you to make better trading decisions without messing up your trading screen. Indicators always lag the actual price action. Thus, we recommend every trader and investor to learn the *Breaker Candle Technique.*

With the help of this technique, you will be able to identify the high and low points of any trend. This will help you maximize your profits and minimize your losses. This technique will save you from traps laid by big players for retail traders, and protect you from false trends and breakouts.

The Rise of the Stock Market

What comes to your mind when you hear the words 'Stock Market?'

Do you feel scared because of your parent's stories about how the stock market destroys everything? Or do you feel excited because a few of your friends have made a lot of money in the stock market?

I had always wondered during my college days what the stock markets actually does. What do they sell? How do they impact the economy? What is their importance? Why are people so crazy about it? Why do they pop up on every news channel I watch?

The short answers to all of these questions lie in the story that I'm going to share with you. Ghanshyam is a well-known fruit seller in the local market. He has made good profits over the past few years. But now he has bigger aspirations. He decides to open a new fruit shop in the neighboring village, to make his fruits available to the villagers, and of course to increase his profits. He goes to the bank and tries to get a loan, but the bank says it's too risky.

He must look at other options. He can go public, giving anyone the opportunity to invest in his business, through something called an Initial Public Offering or IPO. Investors pay a certain amount, say Rs 1000, to own a small part or share of Ghanshyam's business. Ghanshyam sells several shares and grows his fruit business.

Ghanshyam can use this surplus money to open new fruit shops, which means more profits. He can also use some of his profits to develop new products, let's say different varieties of fruits. He can also give some of this money back to his investors. These are called dividends.

He doesn't have to do this, but it does help get people like Raju excited about his business and encourage them to buy his stock. Raju was sick on IPO day, but he believes that Ghanshyam is the smartest businessman in the whole world, and he's certain that his fruit business is going to be huge. So he offers to buy some shares from one of the original investors for twice the actual price he paid for them. Raju believes that if Ghanshyam continues to grow his business, he can sell these shares at an even higher price in the future.

That's the stock market for you.

It comprises people buying and selling tiny pieces of companies and businesses based on how much they think those pieces will be worth in the future. In real life, this happens thousands of times a second, all over the world.

We have 60 major stock exchanges across the world, and Rs 60,000 crores are traded on stock markets in India every day. An average of 20 lakh trades take place every day. But, of course, it didn't start this way. There were many stages along the road to get to our current system of stock exchanges. You may be surprised to learn that the first stock exchange thrived for decades without a single stock being traded.

In the 1600s, the Dutch, British, and French governments gave an 'Article of Incorporation' (a written document establishing a company as a corporation and detailing its governance, structure, and operations) to companies with 'East India' in their names. In the 1600s, everyone seemed to have a stake in the profits from the East Indies and Asia, except the people living there. Sea voyages that brought back goods from the East were extremely risky. Apart from the risk of being attacked by pirates, there were the more common risks of inclement weather and poor navigation.

To lessen the risk of a lost ship ruining their fortunes, ship owners had long been in the practice of seeking investors who would put up money for the voyage, outfitting the ship and crew in return for a percentage of the proceeds if the voyage was successful.

These early companies in the 1600s often lasted for only a single voyage. They were then dissolved, and a new one was created for the next voyage. Investors realized that putting all their eggs into one basket was not a smart way to approach investment in East Indies trading. Let's say that a ship returning from the East Indies had a 33% chance of being seized by pirates. Instead of investing in one voyage and risking the loss of all invested money, investors could purchase shares in multiple companies. Even if one ship was lost out of three or four invested companies, the investor would still make a profit.

When the East India companies were formed, they changed the way business was done. These companies issued stock that would pay dividends on all the proceeds from all the voyages the companies undertook, rather than going voyage by voyage. These were the first modern joint-stock companies (a business owned by its investors, with each investor owning a share of the company based on the amount that they've invested). This allowed the companies to demand more for their shares and build larger fleets. The size of the companies, combined with Royal Charters forbidding competition, meant huge profits for investors. (A Royal Charter is an instrument of incorporation, granted by the King, which confers independent legal personality on an organization and defines its objectives, constitution and powers to govern its own affairs).

Because the shares in the various East India companies were issued on paper, investors could sell the papers to other investors. Unfortunately, there was no stock exchange in existence, so the investor would have to track down a broker to carry out a trade. In other words, coffee shops were the first real stock markets due to the fact that investors would visit these markets to buy and sell stocks. Before long, somebody realized that the entire business world would be more efficient if somebody made a dedicated marketplace where businessmen could trade stocks without having to order a coffee or yell across a crowded café.

On May 17, 1792, the New York Stock Exchange opened under a buttonwood tree in New York City, as 24 stockbrokers signed the Buttonwood Agreement, agreeing to trade five securities under that buttonwood tree. The New York Stock Exchange was not the first stock exchange in the US, however. That honor goes to the Philadelphia Stock Exchange, but the NYSE quickly became the most powerful. The exchange's location, more than anything else, led to the dominance that the NYSE quickly attained. It was in the heart of all the business and trade coming to and going from the United States. It also served as the domestic base for most banks and large corporations.

The Bombay Stock Exchange was started by Premchand Roychand in 1875. While BSE Limited is now synonymous with Dalal Street, it was not always so. In the 1850s, five stock brokers gathered together under a banyan tree in front of Mumbai Town Hall, where Horniman Circle is now situated. A decade later, the brokers moved their location to another leafy setting, this time under banyan trees at the junction of Meadows Street and what was then called Esplanade Road, now Mahatma Gandhi Road. With a rapid increase in the number of brokers, they had to shift places repeatedly. At last, in 1874, the brokers found a permanent location, the one that they could call their own.

The Bombay Stock Exchange continued to operate out of a building near the Town Hall until 1928. The present site near Horniman Circle was acquired by the exchange in 1928, and a building was constructed and occupied in 1930. The street on which the site is located came to be called Dalal Street in Hindi (broker street) due to the location of the exchange.

Today, virtually every country in the world has its own stock market. In the developed world, major stock markets typically emerged in the 19th and 20th centuries soon after the London Stock Exchange and New York Stock Exchange were first created. From Switzerland to Japan, all of the world's major economic powers have highly-developed stock markets which are still active today.

Importance and Impact of Stock Markets on the Economy

The stock market gives opportunities to businesses and the public to transfer capital and ownership in a controlled, secure and managed environment. In addition to providing a convenient way for companies to raise capital and for individuals to increase wealth, the stock market helps keep a check on corporate regulation and increases the economic growth and prosperity of the nation.

Stock markets exist to serve the wider economy. It helps individuals earn a profit on their income when they invest in the stock market and allows firms to spread their risks and receive large rewards. It also enables the government to increase spending through the tax revenue they earn from corporations that trade on the stock exchange. The government uses the revenue to increase re-investment and employment capacity. The stock market plays an important role in the economy of a country in terms of spending and investment. Without stock markets, many countries would not be as developed as they are. Alongside this, it has helped individuals become wealthy and increased the overall standard of living in many economies.

If stock markets did not exist, companies would have to resort to borrowing from the bank to raise money for expansion. This would be a burden on the company as they would have to repay the loans with interest. Fortunately, with stock markets, businesses have the ability to create an IPO and raise large amounts of cash without having to worry about repayment. Moreover, publicly traded companies have no obligation to pay dividends when they incur losses. Capital raised this way can help companies expand operations and create jobs in the economy. From a greater economic perspective, consumer spending increases, governments can benefit from tax revenues and there will be lower levels of unemployment.

One of the most important benefits of the stock market is its ability to help generate personal wealth in the economy. For the individual investor, the stock market provides a way to invest his income to earn a share of the company's profits. The revenue he earns can increase spending in the economy which can have a multiplier effect. The increased spending by individuals leads to increased investment and employment.

One of the key drivers of Gross Domestic Product is the level of investment in the economy. Governments often create fiscal and monetary policies in the economy to promote greater investment. The stock market is considered to be one of the most prominent sources for people to invest money in. Furthermore, investors are always looking to invest in companies with high growth potential. If the stock market is performing well, this not only increases investment from local investors but also attracts foreign direct investment as people abroad invest in the local stock exchange. For example, people in India can invest in the NYSE which helps increase the GDP of the US economy or vice-versa. The performance of the stock market is a rough indicator of how well the economy is performing. This often depends on speculators and the perceptions of investors in the market. A rise or fall in the price of shares represents what cycle the economy is in such as a recession or a boom. There is a direct relationship between the state of the economy and the performance of the stock market. Economists use this as a way to analyse the past performance of investment and spending which helps them in the creation of new economic policies. The stock market serves as a barometer for the economy.

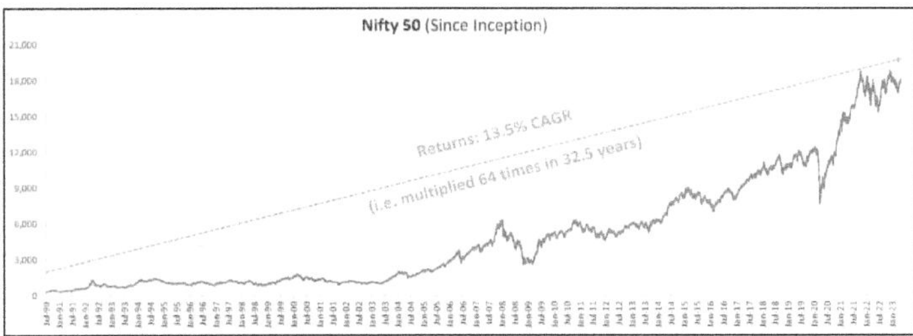

Source: Wealth Conversations Report, May 2023

Your Takeaway

HOW STOCK MARKETS WORK?

Stock markets provide a secure and regulated environment where market participants can transact in shares and other eligible financial instruments with confidence, with zero to low operational risk. Operating under the defined rules as stated by the regulator, the stock markets act as primary markets and secondary markets.

As a primary market, the stock market allows companies to issue and sell their shares to the public for the first time through the process of an IPO. This activity helps companies raise necessary capital from investors.

A company divides itself into several shares and sells some of those shares to the public at a price per share. To facilitate this process, a company needs a marketplace where these shares can be sold and this is achieved by the stock market. A listed company may also offer new, additional shares through other offerings at a later stage, such as through rights issues, which they may even buy back.

Investors will own company shares expecting the share value to rise or dividend payments or both. The stock exchange acts as a facilitator for this capital-raising process and receives a fee for its services from the company and its financial partners using the stock exchanges. Investors can also buy and sell securities they already own in what is called the secondary market.

Most nations have a stock market, and each is regulated by a local financial regulator, monetary authority, or institute. The Securities and Exchange Board of India (SEBI) is the regulatory authority of

Indian Stock exchanges, established under the SEBI Act, 1992 and is the principal regulator for Capital Markets.

Who are the Players

There are three categories of players: Institutional traders, dealers and retail traders. Players of each category have different roles and duties in the market and need to follow certain regulations implemented by SEBI. The institutional traders, whom we will refer to as 'whales', are more involved in the long-term cycle of the market, whereas the dealers are more focused on short-term cycles. We will refer to them as 'sharks'.

Institutional traders

An institutional trader is a member of an institution such as a mutual fund, pension fund, hedge fund, or bank that trades large volumes of securities for the accounts managed by the institution, thus qualifying for preferential treatment and lower commission. This type of trader differs from an individual or retail trader, who trades securities for their personal account.

They buy large quantities of shares and spend a lot of money on these investments. An example of an institutional trader in India is Foreign Institutional

Investors (FII). The institutional investor gets preferential treatment in that the commission is low. Institutional investors face fewer protective regulations from both the government and the regulator since it is assumed that they are more knowledgeable and know how to protect themselves better than retail investors. Other examples of institutional investors include pension funds, life insurance corporations or any institution that makes huge investments.

Market maker

Basically, a market maker's job is to provide liquidity for people at all times. Let's say we're trading a commodity or stock called ABC. The market maker's job is to ensure that there is enough liquidity in the stock such that any person can buy or sell the stock.

The market maker's job is to always provide reasonably-sized liquidity. There is a pre-agreed size for this as well. So, whatever this scenario is, anyone can come in and sell it.

Let's say you have a bid price of Rs 99.50 and the asking price is Rs 100.00. This is the price you are offering the stock at as a market maker. There may be other participants trading this stock and the spread may reduce as more people enter the market to trade this stock.

As the market maker, we are going to offer to sell 1000 shares at Rs 100.00 each and we are going to offer to buy 1000 shares at Rs 99.50 each. So, the market maker always offers to buy and sell.

They might say, okay, I've sold some shares at Rs 100.00 But now my asking price is Rs 100.50. Let's say, this gets filled again. Now the market maker is at 2,000 shares short of the average between the two – Rs 100.00 and Rs 100.50. They might decide to get more aggressive with their bid. They might push the bid price up to Rs 100.30. They will still make some money on this because the average price is Rs 100.25. So, they will offer to buy 2,000 shares at Rs 100.30.

They can adjust the size they want. While there will always be a minimum size they must offer, they can adjust it. They are hoping that ultimately, they can buy back those shares that they sold, and they can constantly make the spread in between. Market makers are very good at this and they are very good at knowing the volatility of the market.

Prop desk

What is proprietary trading or prop trading as it is called? I am looking at it from the perspective of an office of traders that would have employees like you and me coming in, as opposed to a bank which may have a section.

A prop trading firm basically says, if you are really good, you can come and trade my money. But let me see if you are any good first. They might have a few criteria based on which you place trades and prove your expertise. You may have to go through their own training program. If you do well in the training program, they could move you to the prop desk, or they may want to see your statements to ascertain your performance. How much money have you made? Basically, they want to see that you can make them some money. That is the business they are in.

Generally, if you can make the firm some money, they will give you more money to trade with, just like a business would invest in another business and say, hey, I like your business model. Here's some money. I'm expecting to get a return on my money.

They will first examine whether you are a good bet to bet on. This is the risk they take so they must do their due diligence on you. They check your strategy, check the weaknesses in your strategy, interview you, and do various other checks before they say okay.

A good prop deal will get better and better with time, and so will the risk. They will encourage you to trade more. More trades mean more profit. More profit means a good name in the market and additional money.

Price Discovery System

Who actually decides the price of any stock? This question came to mind when I started my trading journey. Who decides how much a stock is worth? How can I know the price of this stock or any other instrument in future? Will it go up or down in value? You may have several such questions when assessing a stock.

Let's understand how a stock price is actually derived. First, you must know that there is no single person who decides the price of a stock. It is decided purely based on the supply and demand. For a trade to take place, a buyer and seller must agree on a price. When they execute the trade, that price becomes the price of the stock. So whatever the last traded price of any stock is, it becomes the current price. Let's understand with an example: A buyer has agreed to purchase a particular stock at Rs 99.00 (bid price) and a seller has agreed to sell that particular stock at Rs 101.00 (ask price). As there is no agreement over the price, the stock price is still the last transaction price. So how does the price change? Let's say we have a set of sellers willing to sell at Rs 101.00, 102.00, 103.00 and 104.00, we have a set of buyers willing to buy at Rs 99.00, 98.00, 97.00, and 96.00. As there is no agreement, there's no movement in price. When a buyer and seller agree on the same price, the price moves. Now let's say you get a clearer picture and are willing to buy the stock at the best price available, i.e. Rs 101.00. A new price has been set for the stock. However, if you have decided to purchase the stock at a price that is not more than Rs 95.00, then you wait in a queue to purchase the stock when a seller offers to sell at this desired price.

When the price moves up fast, it means buyers are eager to purchase the stock at any available price, and obviously, sellers are happy to get the best price for their stock.

Another scenario is that of Gap. A sudden news report that is released after the market closes leads to a gap when the market opens the next day. Again it's the same situation; both the buyers and sellers agree on what they believe to be the new price of the stock after the news report is released.

So, there is no single person or group of persons who decides the price of the stock. The stock price purely depends on how buyers and sellers interact. If enough people believe that the price will go up, and they buy that stock regardless of price, it will go up. If enough people believe that the stock price will go down and they sell aggressively, the price will go down.

Role of Demand and Supply

The stock market also offers a fascinating example of the laws of supply and demand in real-time. For every stock transaction, there must be a buyer and a seller. Because of the immutable laws of supply and demand, if there are more buyers for a specific stock than there are sellers, the stock price will trend up. Conversely, if there are more sellers of the stock than buyers, the price will trend down.

The bid-ask or bid-offer spread, the difference between the bid price for a stock and its ask or offer price, represents the difference between the highest price that a buyer is willing to pay or bid for a stock and the lowest price at which a seller is offering the stock.

A trade transaction occurs either when a buyer accepts the asking price or a seller takes the bid price. If buyers outnumber sellers, they may be willing to raise their bids to acquire the stock. Sellers will, therefore, ask higher prices for it, moving the price up. If sellers outnumber buyers, they may be willing to accept lower offers for the stock, while buyers will also lower their bids, effectively forcing the price down.

Some stock markets rely on professional traders to maintain continuous bids and offers since a motivated buyer or seller may not find each other at any given moment. These are known as specialists or market makers.

A two-sided market consists of the bid and the offer, and the spread is the difference in price between the bid and the offer. The narrower the price spread and the larger the size of the bids and offers, the greater the liquidity of the stock. If there are many buyers and sellers at sequentially higher and lower prices, the market is said to have good depth.

Why the Stock Market Crashes

Stock market crashes are an unavoidable side effect of any market where public perceptions play a role.

Most major stock markets have experienced crashes at some point in history. Stock market crashes are by nature preceded by speculative economic bubbles. A stock market crash can occur when speculations are stretched far beyond the actual value of a stock.

There have been a number of major crashes throughout history, including Black Thursday or Terrible Thursday of 1929, which was followed by Black Monday and Black Tuesday. During this crash, the Dow Jones Industrial Average lost 50% of its value, sending America and much of the world into a deep economic depression and wiping out billions of dollars.

Other major stock market crashes include:

The Stock Market Crash of 1973-1974

Black Monday of 1987

Dot-com Bubble of 2000

Stock Market Crash of 2008

All of these crashes pale in comparison to 1929 but still involved double-digit percentage losses around the world. The advance of electronic trading has caused many to question the foundations of the stock market, including the theory of rational human conduct, the theory of market equilibrium, and the efficient market hypothesis.

The stock market crash of 1987 was the first major crash of the electronic trading era and it was notable because nobody really saw it coming. It was not predated by major news announcements or world affairs. Instead, it seemed to have just happened with no immediately apparent visible reasons.

The 1987 crash began in Hong Kong, where stock markets fell 45.5% between October 19 and October 31. By the end of October, major stock markets around the world had all experienced double-digit collapses. Markets in Australia experienced a 42% drop for example, while the United States and Canada both suffered losses of about 23%.

Your Takeaway

Why Do Only 1% of Investors Make a Fortune?

The title of this chapter is deliberately provocative. We are not particularly interested in why people fail at trading and fail at life. We are more interested in people who don't.

I have been doing this for years and I have met hundreds of people over the course of my career.

Hopefully, I can impart the things I have learned from them to you.

There is sometimes a bit of an aura around professionals in financial markets. This is true to some extent, but there are some idiots as well. Luckily, for me, I have learned more from the mistakes of others than I have from successful traders. I'm here to help you create some success moving forward.

If you are going to take this seriously rather than just a hobby, you will turn it into a profitable undertaking. One thing will lead to the other. People we have mentored through the Sachin Bhatia Equity Research brought up some pretty poignant representations. It is neither corny nor cynical to say that these people have changed their trading style and their lives for the better. With a hundred per cent conviction I can say they have done it because they had a good work ethic and they wanted to be successful.

It is just as important to know how to survive, how to avoid the behavioral traits of people who have lost money, and how to put an end to your losses. There is nothing wrong with seeking out profitable people and emulating their strategies. Being a copycat may get you kicked out of university but it doesn't get you kicked out of the markets.

It is an absolute fallacy for people to think that to succeed in this business you must be a genius. I don't consider myself to be a genius. I have done okay for myself. I had my ups and downs just like everybody else. The one thing I have in common with successful people is a good work ethic. We consistently work hard and learn from our mistakes. We consider investing in the stock market as a business, a consistent and profitable business.

Some personality traits of successful people you may recognize in yourself. I do recognize those personality traits in myself. What is important to understand is that it's not a hack.

This business is not like becoming a dentist. You don't go to university to learn how to drill teeth and then get handed a license. It doesn't work that way. If you think this is just a hack, go do something else. You will certainly make more money elsewhere.

"Skeptical stock traders stay alive and cynical traders suffer from paralysis."

There is no room for cynicism in this business. You either believe that you can do it or you don't. Have you ever been in a boxing ring? Do you feel like you are going to lose the fight the minute you step in? Perhaps you do feel this way if you are cynical about this business. We get plenty of cynical people attending these seminars. *Oh, it's too hard! You know what, you were born 15 years after me. It was great in the early 2000s.* There are no excuses. The job is pretty simple. You get a piece of paper every day with a number at the bottom and your job is to make that number bigger. It's as simple as that. I'm not saying it is that easy to get there, but you must cut the crap. This is what it's all about. If you think that it's too hard, do something else; you are wasting your time in this business.

Skepticism is not cynicism. It is important to be skeptical. Being skeptical is what keeps people away from dubious schemes like Bitcoin and various other stock market frauds and melodious business models which are propagated by the financial press. Being skeptical is totally okay, but being cynical is not going to take you anywhere. Have you ever met a cynical trader? I have never met a wealthy cynical trader. Remove cynicism from your thought process and remove cynical people from your trading life. They will prevent you from making money. They make themselves feel better by dragging you down. There is no room for them in your life. There is no need for you to be with them.

An unwillingness to manage risk always ends badly. I don't think I need to expand on this point. Every trader has lost money at some point in time due to an inability to manage risk. Learn how to manage risk. It is not the most difficult part of this job.

"The conscientious trader will always outearn the lazy genius"

I believe this wholeheartedly. If you have a good work ethic and apply what you know, you will outperform an idle genius. There aren't too many things in the world where we can say this, but trust me, I've seen it happen again and again. I have seen geniuses with no work ethic fail miserably at this business.

There are a couple of parallels to losing in trading and losing in life. Hopefully, we can avoid them. We know there is no hack but what is there? There is education and understanding. Plenty of studies have shown that you can increase your IQ with adequate education. Idea generation happens with experience and then there is the application of these ideas.

Based on the people I've worked with and mentored, most are better at the idea-generation process than they think. Most people have ideas, but it is in the application of their ideas – turning a thought bubble into something that is profitable – that they falter.

Plenty of people I know behave this way. Most people have ideas and can generate them easily. But how do you turn an idea that sounds intuitively correct into something that can actually put some money in your pocket? Someone asked me why these hedge funds have models and processes. It helps turn an idea into money. This is what we are trying to teach people. The process needs to be consistent and repeatable. You need to write your ideas down and turn them into something that can help you make money.

Distraction

What are our biggest distractions? Falling in love with potential outcomes and ignoring the pathways. What do you think about that? I don't know what you're into, but if you want to drive a Ferrari, be surrounded by good-looking people, have a big house, a helicopter, you cannot fall in love with potential outcomes without having any strategies in place to get there. It is very common for many of these financial institutions to prey upon our aspirations through their advertising and internet memes where people are driving around with bundles of cash in Italian sports cars.

It's fine to have hopes and dreams, but there must be a clear path to get there. How do you make the number at the bottom of the page bigger every day, every week, every month, and every year? The pathway is unavoidable. If you get the outcomes you want, it's awesome. But this is not what this business is about. It takes a while to get to where you want to be with any business. It's absolutely true of this business as well. Yet, people are prepared to do stupid things with their money in the stock market every single day. It is perplexing why people can't see this as a business because that's exactly what it is.

Social media is the biggest distraction in most people's lives. Why do you think people get paid millions of dollars a year to come up with web content which keeps you hot? It doesn't make you any money. Social media is there to be used; don't let it use you. Unfortunately, many people fall into the trap of using social media thinking that it is going to help them. Four hours later, they're looking at pictures of cats on Facebook. It is there to distract you; it is not there to make you money. But if you want to use social media, you can make it work for you.

Analysis is not storytelling. What do we focus on in this business? What do we focus on incorporating into our process? Numbers.

If you are not competent or confident with basic arithmetic, then learn it because it is unavoidable. Stories are great but there is a quantitative element to this business which you simply can't avoid. You need to get your head around it. It is not that difficult.

Awareness

What must the successful trader be aware of? He must be aware of everything that involves stocks, commodities, and currencies. Develop a filter; it can be hard, but you need to do it. Prices are everything, as I mentioned before. Information has never been more readily available to the retail trader. Much of this information might be crap. We know this, but nonetheless, it is still there. The point is, if you want to be wilfully ignorant, if you don't like reading, if you don't like accumulating information, just do something else; don't waste your time in this business.

What is the opposite of being wilfully ignorant? It is being curious. Be a perpetual learner. Willingly investigate and do research on the details. Three personality traits have helped me very well throughout my career. To anyone who is a perpetual learner, you need to enjoy the learning process, stay on top of the numbers, learn about the stocks, commodities and bonds, and be willing to learn something every single day. If you can't get your head into this space, do something else.

Academic rigor

People from finance and mathematics view the markets as a series of problems that need to be solved. Many of us, myself included, who have spent five years doing something in finance that has a vague quantitative element, believe we have a good knowledge foundation, and there are not too many gaps that need to be filled. This is not true. I have met people with a master's degree who are not smart enough to deal with the markets. I'm not denigrating formal education at all. There is an element of understanding which people really do need to have. But what I want to bring to your attention is that it is very difficult for practitioners in traditional educational establishments to impart knowledge of the real world of trading. I'm not saying that they lack IQ or academic prowess. It just boils down to the fact they haven't actually traded in the market. The point I'm trying to make is that some quantitative skills and the desire to apply a critical set of thoughts to the market are invaluable skills. Not everyone has such skills but it is invaluable. You can develop it though.

In high school, if you are dissecting a frog or heating a milliliter of water, you are always taught to go through the experiment in a repeatable and consistent manner. The core of what we are trying to teach people in this business is to have a consistent and repeatable process.

Bad luck

If you have no ideas, you have nothing. Where do you start on your very first day of working out how to trade a stock? You have to start somewhere. If your strategy is not working, don't attribute it to bad luck. There's a problem with your strategy and this needs to be addressed. There may be a bit of bad luck here and there, but generally, it's not the case. If you have a process which is consistent and repeatable you should be able to go back, revise the work that you have done and pinpoint the mistake that you made. That is the point of this whole exercise. That is the point of having some financial education instead of throwing darts in the dark. You should know what to do when things go wrong and how to deal with difficult situations.

Anybody can high-five their friends when things are going well. When they are winning, everything is fine. Unfortunately, there are not many lessons learned when winning because people tend to put that down to their own good judgment rather than what is often their own good luck. But there are many lessons to be learned when losing money. Having a process allows you to go back, and hopefully, you will not make the same mistake again. You will also learn from your mistakes. This is why I'm a big advocate of having a step-by-step process in this business.

Unfortunately, nothing teaches us a lesson more than losing in the market. Most people can probably relate to this. People without a process cannot, because they don't know where they went wrong. They will put it down to bad luck or nebulous concepts which are generally wrong. I'm talking more about equities in this instance. It's very important to anyone's process, though it's largely the most basic as well. Quantitative finance is probably the most difficult discipline in this industry to succeed in.

The point I'm trying to make is that the quantitative side of it is important. But, over time, it will actually become the simplest part of your job. It involves getting over the hump, a bit of practice and repetition. Initially, it is quite complex, but after a while, it becomes second nature.

Risk management

Risk management is not about avoiding risks, but about taking calculated risks. Paradoxically, the biggest risk is never taking any risk in the first place. Most people can probably relate to this. I'm not trying to get all deep and meaningful, but it's pretty easy to go through life taking huge risks if your outcome is pretty much known from day one.

Knowledge is the ultimate risk management. Once again, the point is you know what to do when things go wrong. You might wonder why this crazy man from the other side of the world is continually stressing about the process. The truth is, without a process, you are throwing darts in the dark. You are flipping coins to make decisions. This whole thing is designed to ensure that the odds are in your favor. It is not a game of chance; it is a game of analysis and hard work. The trader with no process is like the blind squirrel who occasionally finds enough food.

Demo accounts

I didn't realize they existed until a couple of years ago. I don't understand it and frankly, I don't want to talk about it. You can't pay your bills using a demo account. People need to understand the emotional reactions associated with winning and losing money. Even if it's a very small amount of money, even if it is just Rs 2000, at least you can go to a restaurant with your friend and talk about it.

What is the point of a demo account? It is just another procrastination tool or a distraction which is literally worthless. But it seems like an incredibly popular undertaking for people. I just don't get it.

Numbers don't get happy, sad or angry. Focus on them before you delve into the story and there's always a story. Focus on the numbers.

Common traits

What are the common traits of the emotional and subjective trader? Unfortunately, people reading this book might see these traits in themselves. If you see these traits in yourself, deep down you know that you need to eradicate them. If you don’t see these traits in yourself, you either don't have them, which is great, or there's something wrong. Many people cannot be bothered to objectively expand their knowledge. Plenty of people are like this. They love to be wilfully ignorant. People don't want to know the truth. They are wedded to certain ideas, despite these ideas being demonstrably wrong. How many people have told you to buy bitcoins over the last few years when it's been witnessing a painful death by a thousand cuts bare market? Why can’t they just accept that they're wrong? They just need to get over it. Some people turn a blind eye to the fact that they're losing money.

If you see these traits in yourself get rid of them. It is an express train to the poorhouse and it is surprisingly common. Hopefully, you are not one of those people who are unable to accept criticism and are hostile to new ideas. When you own a stock that's going up and every bit of news you receive about that stock is positive, does it give you a warm feeling inside? Of course, it does, but it doesn't really get you anywhere. You're almost better off reading research when it contradicts your own views. There's information in that. Confirmation bias is extremely dangerous. Many professional investors I've come across suffer from this bias more so than retail investors, because they think they're very smart. There are certain character traits a lot of people on the buy side exhibit when stockbrokers are calling them daily and telling them how good they are. All they are really doing is indulging in confirmation bias every day. People are totally and utterly in love with this. It is dangerous. If you see this personality trait in yourself, eradicate it. Save yourself some money.

What is a market? What's the definition of a market? There are many definitions, but the one below is the most concise and apt.

"It is the money-weighted sum of people's expectations."

There are thousands of people that participate in the stock market every day. There are a hundred different mandates every day. There are technology changes on a constant basis. There are changes in the speed of communication and there are changes in the performance of all companies themselves. How is it possible that such a market won't change over time? It has to. People wonder why the rules that came into force in the 1920s don't work today.

The most expensive words in history: This time it is different. It sounds pretty good, doesn't it?

It is different every day. How can it not be? Markets continually evolve. If you can't accept this, once again, go do something else. You will make more money elsewhere. Don't waste your time in this business.

So what are the common traits of reasonable and objective people who in my experience tend to make more money? They are willing to discuss both sides of the argument. If you can't listen to both sides of the argument you're destined to fail.

Adaptability

Accept that things will change. Accept that you will make mistakes. Markets tend not to treat perfectionists very well. It is great to have a high winning percentage; it is great to be good at what you do, but if you are a perfectionist, the reality is you probably need to get over it to some extent, because you are going to make mistakes. I have made more mistakes than I can count. Most professional investors who speak the truth will tell you the same thing. But I know when to cut such things quickly. But there will be mistakes. The point is, don't make the same mistake more than once. Profitability speaks for itself.

Your Takeaway

Common Beliefs about the Stock Market

Many investors wonder whether they should invest in stocks. Before deciding to invest, it's important to have an accurate understanding of stocks and trading rather than blindly accepting common myths. You should overcome investing myths to improve your investing decisions. There are a few common myths that most people believe to be true. Here are five of these myths and the truth behind them.

Myth-1: You Need to Diversify

You need to diversify: This is not true but you might have heard this a lot, especially from financial advisors and professional investors.

You need 20 stocks in your portfolio. You need 200 stocks in your portfolio. The reason they believe this is because they all follow a strategy that is commonly taught in all business schools. It is the Modern Portfolio Theory that basically says that the only way to reduce systemic risk is to diversify into a lot of companies, like 20, 30, or 40 different companies. This is just garbage. It is not true. The only reason that you really need to diversify is if you don't know what you are doing. This is not an attack on people who are diversified in an index fund. If you are investing in an index fund, you accept that you are not confident about what you are doing. You are just accepting the market returns; you don't want to invest in individual businesses.

However, if you are investing in individual businesses, then you must not over diversify and I will explain why. You certainly don't want to put all your eggs in one basket as Warren Buffet says. It may not be a good idea to just invest your entire net worth into one stock and pray that this stock does really well over time. On the contrary, if you invest in more than 10 to 15 stocks, you are not going to have enough time to study these stocks in depth.

You could choose to know a little bit about several stocks and make a lot of bad picks. Instead, what you should do is pick around two to three stocks at a time, so that you can study them extensively for months at a time and learn every single detail about them. Make sure that you are only making good investments. You don't want to invest in ten rubbish stocks that are not going to do you any good.

If you invest in 10 average stocks it will not perform well. It doesn't matter that you have diversified. However, if you pick stocks that you have studied and you are totally confident about where those companies are going in the future, then you are going to do a lot better than the person who just over-diversifies and barely knows anything about the stocks they buy.

If you have picked 10 stocks and there are a couple that you really believe in and you have some money to invest, why would you invest that money in your

20th or 30th best idea? Why wouldn't you want to put more money into your number one pick, the pick that you really believe in?

Myth-2: You Need to be Clever to Invest

There is a misconception that you need to spend hours and hours researching stocks, analyzing these companies, and understanding balance sheets if you want to start investing. The world of finance is filled with a lot of jargon.

I admit this can be quite intimidating, especially if you are not in this field. Sometimes, I feel this jargon is just there to stop people from investing and taking control of their own personal finances. It makes people feel like they don't really understand the investing business. So they either stay clear or pay someone else to do it for them because it's far easier to do so. I do think that there is definitely space for professionals to exist in this field or any other field. But it is important that you know how to handle it and understand it yourself. With regards to personal finance, you don't need to go to a financial advisor to start investing. You don't need to understand every detail of a financial statement to start investing. It is not about doing extensive research on numerous stocks, having good instincts or knowing what's happening in every single industry. It involves understanding the basic principles of investing to get started and then being disciplined to keep going.

Myth-3: Percentage Gains Equals Percentage Losses

People make this mistake very often. Understanding percentage gains and losses over time is super important if you are looking to get into investing or are already investing, as it helps you determine your rate of return or net gain or loss over a period.

Most people believe that the percentage gain is equivalent to the percentage loss. Say you were down 5% yesterday and are up 5% today, you may believe that you are at the same level that you were two days ago, but this is not actually correct.

If you started with Rs 10,000 two days ago and you lose 5% of this, then you have Rs 9,500 left. Now, if you gain 5% on this Rs 9,500 that you have, you have only Rs 9970 left.

So our minds can easily trick us. If your stock has fallen by 5%, then it will need to increase by 5.26% to get to that same price as before.

Percentage Loss	Return back to break-even
5 %	5.26 %
10 %	11.11 %
20 %	25 %
30 %	42.86 %
40 %	66.67 %
50 %	100 %
60 %	150 %
70 %	233.34 %
80 %	400 %
90 %	900 %

Myth-4: Buy the Dip

Prices fall when there's a market crash or a market correction. Most stocks go on sale. but buying every stock simply because the price has fallen is not a good strategy. Suppose you are looking at two stocks. Stock A reached an all-time high last year at around Rs 500. It has fallen to Rs 100 per share. You also have Stock B. It is a smaller company, but recently, its price went up from Rs 100 to Rs 150 per share. Which stock should you buy?

The majority of investors would choose stock A, the stock that has fallen from Rs 500 to Rs 100 because they believe it will eventually make its way back up to those levels again. Thinking this way is one of the cardinal sins of investing and we often do this without even realizing it. Research shows that people are more likely to buy something when it is on sale than if it was marketed at that discounted price to start with. That's because our brains are wired to think that the quality and value of the item that we are getting is actually closer to the original higher price.

So, we think we are getting a bargain, but the price is only a small part of the equation. The goal is not to just buy stocks that are heavily discounted for the sake of it. Instead, the goal is to buy high-quality growth companies at a reasonable price.

Myth-5: Investing is Gambling

There is a popular myth that investing in the stock market is just like gambling. People who invest in the financial markets are just speculators and are lucky enough to make money. Although there are a few similar features between trading and gambling, they are very distinct.

The variance in risk and return is the point of distinction between gambling and trading. In stock markets, the yield may be greater than the risk, while the risk is greater than the yield in gambling. Stock markets encourage us to be both a buyer and seller, while you can only be a buyer in gambling. Given the above, people mainly lose money in the stock markets because they put money into stocks without any real knowledge or analytical skills. If you treat stock trading like gambling, it certainly becomes a gamble for you.

In the stock market, you have an edge called statistical advantage. The key to success is doing continuous research; you make informed decisions. Whereas in gambling, you more or less depend on the luck factor. Trading will be similar to gambling when you just pick random stocks and make transactions.

When you invest in something to generate profits, it becomes a business. In businesses or trading, the reward-to-risk ratio is high. People lose money only when they fail to understand the risk-to-reward ratio before arriving at any decision. In gambling, most often it is the dealer (bookmakers and casinos) who makes a profit. You speculate and the odds are never in your favor.

Your Takeaway

YOUR FIRST STEP TOWARD FINANCIAL NIRVANA

Today, the stock market has schools, careers, and even whole television channels dedicated to understanding it. However the modern stock market is significantly more complicated than its original incarnation. So, how do companies and investors use the market today?

Let's imagine a new coffee company that decides to launch in the market. First, the company will advertise itself to big investors. If they think the company is a good idea, they get the first crack at investing, and sponsoring the company's IPO. This launches the company into the official public market, where any company or individual who believes the business can be profitable may buy a stock. Buying stocks makes these investors partial owners of the business. Their investment helps the company to grow, and as it becomes more successful, more buyers may see potential and start buying stocks. As demand for these stocks increases, so does their price, increasing the cost for prospective buyers, and raising the value of the company's stocks people already own. For the company, this increased interest helps fund new initiatives and also boosts its overall market value by showing how many people are willing to invest in their idea. However, if for some reason a company starts to seem less profitable, the reverse can also happen.

If investors think their stock value is going to decline, they will sell their stocks with the hopes of making a profit before the company loses more value. As stocks are sold and demand for the stock goes down, the stock price falls, and with it, the company's market value. This can leave investors with big losses unless the company starts to look profitable again. This see-saw of supply and demand is influenced by many factors. Companies are under the unavoidable influence of market forces such as the fluctuating price of materials, changes in production technology, and the shifting costs of labor. Investors may be worried about changes in leadership, bad publicity, or larger factors like new laws and trade policies. And of course, plenty of investors are simply ready to sell valuable stocks and pursue personal interests.

All these variables cause day-to-day noise in the market, which can make companies appear more or less successful. In the stock market, appearing to lose value often leads to losing investors, and in turn, losing actual value. Human confidence in the market has the power to trigger everything from economic booms to financial crises. And this difficult-to-track variable is why most professionals promote reliable long-term investing over trying to make quick cash. However, experts are constantly building tools in an effort to increase their chances of success in this highly unpredictable system. But the stock market is not just for the rich and powerful. With the dawn of the Internet, everyday investors can buy stocks in many of the exact same ways a large investor can. As more people educate themselves about this complex system, they too can trade stocks, support the businesses they believe in, and pursue their financial goals. The first step is getting started.

If consistent results are your objective, then you must learn how to think like a professional trader. Because that is what they do; they make consistent results. That is why they are pros, that is why people give them their money to manage, and that is why they have jobs. They actually trade for a living because if they didn't get consistent results they wouldn't be able to keep their jobs. To be able to consistently make money, you must learn to change the way you look at trading. You must believe that you are not going to be disappointed or betrayed or suffer emotional pain. You must get to that carefree state of mind. Once you do this, once you shift your perspective, everything changes. It's not about being right or wrong. When you understand that you must go through the process of learning how to accept the risk of losing, then everything about your trading will change.

Overcoming Mental Blocks

> ***Overcoming mental blocks is the foremost favor a trader can do to himself***
>
> **– Ramesh Patra**

If you are a stock market trader, you might have already realized that earning a steady income is not such an easy task. Everyone seems to think that because trading is easy or because it's easy to find yourself in a winning trade, which does happen occasionally, it's easy to become a consistent winner.

It took me a long time to realize that winning and being a consistent winner are two completely different things. In some ways, there isn't even a relationship between the two.

This is a really hard mental barrier to breakthrough, mainly because it's so easy to find yourself in a winning trade, since winning actually requires no skill at all unless you consider clicking a mouse button or tapping a pad to be a complex skill.

So the question arises, if it is that easy to win, it can't be that much harder to make a steady income. What makes consistency so challenging?

The most general answer I can give is, that it requires learning the type of skills that people just aren't used to learning. It requires mental skills. Most people assume that because their technical strategy gives them a signal to get into a trade, and it produces a high percentage of winning trades, it will equate to a consistent income.

They don't take into consideration that the proper execution of these signals requires mental skills.

For example, a high school basketball player goes to the playground and practices his free throw for two to three hours a day. It wouldn't be unusual for him to be able to get 50 free throws into the basket in a row. The question is, will he be able to get two successful free throws in a row if he was in the final game of the UBL Pro League? His team is down one point and there are only a few seconds left on the clock. He fouls and this changes everything. Under these circumstances, without the appropriate mental skills, it will be difficult for him to execute even one free throw. Regardless of how well he could execute it in practice, he is bound to choke in a final game.

With training, we can develop a technical method that will tell us what to do and give us the potential to generate consistent results. But like the basketball player, without developing our mental skills, it is unlikely we will be able to execute our strategies – to stay positively focused on the process of training by doing exactly what we need to do when we need to do it without hesitation, reservation or fear. No matter how good a technical method is for generating winning trades, turning those winners into consistent income requires the ability to do or not do certain things that the method itself can't help us with.

For example, our method can't force us to predefine the risk of getting into a trade. If we do predefine the risk, our method can't force us to accept the loss we end up with. Our method can't prevent us from moving a stop closer to our entry point where we get stopped out, and the market trades back in our favor. Our method can't prevent us from hesitating and getting in too late. Our method can't stop us from jumping the gun and getting in too soon. Our method can't stop us from getting out of a winning trade too soon, leaving money on the table, nor can it prevent us from letting a winning trade turn into a losing trade without making any profit.

All these mental errors I just listed are the result of thinking, believing or assuming that our technical method is telling us what is going to happen next on a trade-by-trade basis without understanding that technical methods are not designed to do that. Technical methods and patterns are designed to put the odds of success in our favor over a series of trades. It may not seem like it on the surface, but there are some profound psychological implications here. What this means is the outcome of the signals generated by any technical method on a trade-by-trade basis is unique and random;

in other words, there's no way to know in advance what the outcome of any particular signal will be, or what the sequence of wins or losses will be over a series of trades.

I know it's somewhat of a paradox to think that events that have a random outcome can produce consistent results. But think about it; this is the principle that has been used by casinos for hundreds of years. Right?

Technical methods and patterns will give the individual trader the same kind of advantage the casino has over the individual player if the trader can look at things with the right perspective. On the other hand, if a trader who has generated his signal from a technical method has learned to integrate this randomness principle with his training regimen, he will undoubtedly find that training can be one of the most frustrating if not exasperating endeavors he has ever chosen to undertake.

You only get frustrated when you don't get the expected results from your technical methods. Technical methods define and identify patterns. The patterns definitely exist and repeat themselves over and over again. The problem is that the outcomes don't always correspond with the patterns on a trade-by-trade basis. What I'm saying is that yes we have patterns, yes they repeat themselves again and again, and our minds naturally think we will have a pattern that is consistent, so we should have an outcome that is consistent with the pattern. But this is not the case at all. There doesn't have to be a relationship between the outcome and the pattern.

In other words, if the trade I'm in right now turns out to be a winner, does this mean that the next trade is going to be a winner? Absolutely not. The trade I'm in right now can end up being a losing proposition. But does this mean I will lose money in the next trade too?

There is a random distribution between wins and losses over any sequence of trades that you look at. This is a very difficult concept to grasp, but traders have managed to grasp and learn how to think in terms of what I call probabilities. They don't experience the same kind of emotional trauma that the typical trader does because they expect something that just may not happen. For example, if this trade I place right now is a winner, and I apply the exact same criteria to the next trade, I naturally expect it to be a winner. On the other hand, if I face two or three losses in a row, I will naturally expect my next trade to be a loser too.

One of the main reasons why people have such a difficult time understanding this is because their initial exposure to the markets is through an electronic medium. When you trade on a digital platform, there is a real disconnect between the actual trades that are happening and what is causing the price movement. The market started as exchanges and all prices are people-generated events. This is what you must take into consideration: Everything happens because of what people believe. Look at the nature of trading and break it down into its simplest components. What you have is everyone trying to do the same thing. There is no possible way that any of us can make money as traders unless we can buy low and sell high or sell high and buy low. So basically, everyone is trying to do the same thing. The reason why we have price movements is because everyone has a different idea about what is high and what is low.

If you are going to place an order to buy something at Rs 100, it is because you believe that the stock price can go up to Rs 110 or even Rs 120. If I believed the price may go down to Rs 90, I would wait to buy the stock, right? I choose to buy it at Rs 100 because I believe the stock price will go up. All price movements are based on people's beliefs about what is going to happen in the future.

Since all price movements are based on people's convictions or beliefs about the future, how do prices actually move? For example, when I place an order, I don't trade at a level where I can actually move prices. But what the typical screen-based trader does not understand is that there are thousands of traders who do move prices, and it is their intention to move prices. You could also have a large group of traders coming into the market which will cause prices to move. But what must actually happen for prices to move? If the last price of something stands at Rs 10, and the market actually moves to Rs 11, all the offers at Rs 10 must be removed; if the market moves to Rs 12, then all offers at Rs 11 must be removed. In other words, people trying to sell at Rs 11 must get their orders filled before the stock price moves to Rs 12. For someone to actually bid at Rs 11 or Rs 12, they are doing the exact opposite. They are not buying low, they are buying high relative to the last price.

You must understand how prices move because it will help you understand how your technical methods relate to this movement. Technical methods may incorporate visual patterns or moving averages or mathematical formulas. You are considering what people believe about the future and transforming their beliefs into a data point as a price, over time. Arriving at these data points using certain types of mathematical equations will help you identify patterns in collective human behavior and what they mean. When this set of criteria is present in the market, there is simply a higher probability than not of one thing happening over another.

When this collective pattern is present it will repeat itself. But the problem is that it repeats itself on a random basis because even though the actual mathematical criteria is exactly the same, you can't predict human beings. Mathematical models can't predict the actual individuals who will come into the market and trigger price movements.

How does believing in a random result affect your expectations? What you want to avoid is to place a trade with the possibility of being disappointed, dissatisfied or betrayed, because a lot of traders feel this way. When the potential to be betrayed exists, it negatively impacts the way you see market information. In other words, all of us have these mechanisms to avoid mental pain that affect our perception of information. For example, I'm in a losing trade which I entered thinking I was going to win, after doing all my evaluation, analysis, and work to build my case.

As the market moves against me, I will have the tendency to focus on information that tells me that I'm right, ignoring the information that tells me that the market is actually trending against me.

To be consistent, the principle that we need to keep in mind is that we must cut our losses and let our profits run. We must make more on our winning trades and lose less on our losing trades. If I'm susceptible to being disappointed or betrayed, if I get into a trade expecting it to do what I think it should do, I'm going to have this tendency to distort market information that causes me to hang on to my losers. Meanwhile, what will happen in a winning trade is that instead of letting a winner run, I will cut the positions early, before it can shower me with profits.

Regardless of the reason, whether it's a news report or anything else, other traders may not necessarily buy into that reason. They don't have any reason to buy the stock at a price that is worse than yours. You bought the stock at Rs 10, and some people want to buy it at Rs 11, some at Rs 12 and some others at Rs 13. They must remove the offers of all the traders who thought the stock was valued high at these prices. If these people don't participate in the market, then whatever the reason you purchased that stock at that particular price might not be good enough. That is why it is so critical to predefine your risk before you even place a trade. That is also why professional traders don't think about it any other way because they know it involves other people. My reason may be great but if someone else is not buying into it what difference does it make? It doesn't matter because it is not a winning trade.

Trading is not a right or wrong game. It has nothing to do with being right or wrong. Trading is a technical methodology or a technical pattern. It doesn't have anything to do with being right or wrong. It is just an odds game, that is all it is. In other words, you get an edge that says you have the odds in your favor over a series of trades but you must be able to take every single trade because you don't know the sequence of wins and losses. You must be able to identify what your risk is. How much are you willing to spend to find out if other traders will come into the market and bid at a price higher than your price, or offer the stock at a lower price than your selling price? That is all it means. Of course, you must have a money management plan for how to manage consistent profits.

You might wonder if there are any steps you can follow to think like a professional trader. Is it possible to trade from a carefree state of mind? Is it possible to train the mind in such a way so as to cut your losing trades as early as possible and let your winners run?

The answer is a resounding yes. There are exercises on how to think like a professional trader. Basically, all it takes is simply a sincere willingness to do it. It is just like anything else in our lives. When you have a particular goal, and a strong desire to achieve that goal, then you will take whatever steps are necessary to achieve it. If you set your mind to achieving something, you will get there. But first, you must be determined to change your way of thinking. There are so many people who are so close to getting it, but they never really fully understand, because they don't want to change the way they think. You can trade in a free state of mind by changing the way you think. You must eliminate the potential to think that the market is going to disappoint you. The way you eliminate this potential is by understanding that trading is not about being right or wrong, it is a probability game.

There are stages of development where we start out learning the fundamental skills like learning how to think in probabilities so that the market doesn't have the potential to cause us any emotional pain. When you place a trade and it doesn't work, all it really means is that some traders who had the same beliefs as you didn't come into the market. It is nothing more than that, but you must learn to walk away when the odds are not in your favor.

How good do you think the average person is at predicting how other people will behave? No one is good at predicting how other people will behave. They cannot even be certain about their own behavior. So how good can they be at predicting collective human behavior?

The methodologies that we have access to, the mathematical formulas, do this for us. But you must understand that there is no possible way that these mathematical formulas can predict the outcome of these patterns on a trade-by-trade basis. It can predict only on a series of trades.

In other words, what these patterns tell you is that the odds are in your favor, that somebody will come into the market and bid at a higher price than your bid or offer the stock at a lower price than your ask. That is all it says. This is either going to happen or not and there's nothing right or wrong about it. I look at it as how much distance am I willing to give the market to move away from my entry point, to tell me that they will either come or will not, and going any further is not worth the money to find out.

Qualities of a Good Trader

The basic reasons for losing money in the stock market are rules and analysis. Rules and analysis run side by side. How can you survive in the market without analysis? I have seen traders who enter into a trade based on their instinct. This is not trading; it is basically gambling if you don't analyze the market. However, sometimes, over-analysis can create problems. How can you recognize that you are overanalyzing or not? If you get contradictory signals.

If you combine two strategies or indicators, often you will find that whatever signal the first strategy or indicator gives, the second one doesn't support. So, it is recommended that you keep your trading style simple so that you will get a better and clearer picture of the market rather than getting contradictory signals.

To be a retail trader you must be equipped with patience and discipline. There are times when you may need to sit with folded hands. There are times when you must wait for a good trade to appear. As a retail trader, you must not trade round-the-clock like a high-frequency trader.

Your Takeaway

Pioneering Breaker Candle Technique

The Breaker Candle Technique is a technical analysis method where you can make trading decisions fast without the help of any indicator or tool, by only looking at the price actions. In other words, you can see a better and clearer picture of the market and can make better trading decisions with this technique, without making your trading screen look messy.

Why do I recommend that every trader and investor learn the Breaker Candle Technique? There is a time gap between price action and the outcome of an indicator. Indicators are always lagging behind the actual price action that is currently going on. Let's look at the Relative Strength Index (RSI) where the length is 14. How do you calculate the current value of RSI? Let's say that in the last 14 days, or over the latest 14 candles in the timeframe you have selected, there were 10 up days/candles and 4 down days/candles. RSI will take the average gain on the 10 up days and divide it by 14. Then, it will take the average loss of 4 down days and divide it by 14. So, what RSI is basically doing is providing the average sum total of the last 14 candles, depending on the time frame you have selected. However, the actual price action going on at a particular moment is very different from the average 14 candles. If you make a decision based on the average values created by the RSI or any such indicators, it is very difficult for you to take the right decision in a timely manner to align yourself with the actual price action going on.

You can align with the flow of the market if you make a decision on the price actions going on in real-time, rather than focusing on the average of the latest candles. The Breaker Candle Technique helps you make the right decision immediately after any price action happens in the market. It also helps you identify the current market trend, when a new trend will start, when a reversal might occur, where you must put your stop, and up to what price level you should hold your trade. Basically, a retail trader needs to know every detail to make the right decision in the market.

Benefits of Breaker Candle Technique;

Have you ever wondered how your trading screen will look like when you put more than one indicator to make your decision easy? It looks cluttered, right? The problem starts when you get contradictory outcomes from indicators. The purpose of any indicator or tool is to help you take the right decision in real-time, rather than leaving you in a dilemma, because every indicator has its own calculations, depending on the time frame.

What does a retail trader need to make the right decisions in the market? What do you need to be a profitable trader? A systematic process, right? The Breaker Candle Technique is the mother of all price action techniques, which helps retail traders by providing the right information in real-time, without any delay, and without the use of any fancy tools or indicators.

This technique will allow you not to deviate from your decision. All of us have experienced this feeling when we wonder if we should exit from the trade or hold on a little longer. Early exit from profitable trades and re-entering the trades again and again without knowing the right entry points creates unnecessary trauma in a retail trader's mind.

With the help of the Breaker Candle Technique, you will be able to identify the nearly high and low points of any trend. Thus, it helps you in maximizing your profits and minimizing your losses. You will never be stuck in a wrong trade and suffer big losses. This is the ultimate goal of any retail trader.

The Breaker Candle Technique saves you from traps that big players create for retail traders. It saves you from pump-and-dump price actions, false trends, and false breakouts. How? We validate the trends with every third new candle so you get to know what is going on in the market. Is the trend continuing or is it time to book profit? By market I mean any tradable instrument; it might be equity, currencies, or commodities.

What if I tell you that once you become familiar with the Breaker Candle Technique, you don't need to remember any chart patterns or harmonic patterns, because we all know deep down that these patterns are derived from basic price actions. You will know what is going on in the market before any chart patterns are formed on the screen with the help of this technique.

Most importantly, you will not be dependent on any external third party for any trade information. You will know if the market is getting ready for an upside or downside or if it's in the consolidation phase. If you place trades based on someone else's recommendations, you will get to know whether you are on the right or wrong side of the trend.

What Do You Need?

First, you need any charting software like tradingview.com or investing.com to get real-time data. You can get this from your broker too. It can be any charting software where you can see the price movements in real-time.

If you are unable to continuously watch the market movements like a working professional, you must have price-level alert tools so that you don't have to watch the screen continuously. You also need a broker terminal to place orders, unless you call in your trades.

Most importantly, you need the right stock with positive beta and the right volatility. Why the right stocks are very important? As a trader, without any movement in price, how can you make money? You can do it through options selling, but being a new trader, I recommend that you start with the right stocks.

And, of course, you need complete knowledge of the Breaker Candle Technique. You need to practice using it a lot to gain mastery over it.

Patience and discipline are the two major factors in this business of trading. If you panic during trades, like most people do at the beginning of their career in the stock market, you must learn to control your emotions. I talk about the process repeatedly because your process must have an edge which must reduce your panic levels, and allow you to become a disciplined trader. The Breaker Candle Technique is the sum total of the characteristics of a trader. You don't need to learn all this from anywhere else. This technique will do it for you if you can properly follow the rules that will be discussed in the forthcoming chapters.

It is critical that you deal with the right stocks only. How can you identify a good stock? Stocks which are less volatile must be avoided. What does less volatile mean? Let's say a stock moves in one candle, then takes a rest for the next six to ten candles repeatedly. Stocks with low volumes must be avoided, as you will not get the right liquidity for the transactions. Stocks with high volatility, those that move more than 1% with every candle must be avoided, as you can't keep pace with the momentum.

The Breaker Candle Technique is designed to solve all these problems that a trader faces on a daily basis. It can be used on any time frame and on any instrument where candles are formed. But it becomes aggressive for any time frame below 15 minutes or an hour. Let's say, for every minute, you want to analyze what is going on in the market. It will be too aggressive for you. You need to have patience to analyze any stock, instrument or market in the time frame you are comfortable with. You need to know what time frame is most suitable for you, where you can analyze without messing up.

Your Takeaway

IN DEPTH STUDY OF BCT

"A simple and effective method is the best friend of a trader."

As the Breaker Candle Technique is derived from the basic price actions which are unavoidable in the market, it can be your best friend in the market if you apply it correctly in your day-to-day trading. I've talked about the process multiple times so far because I believe it is something that can change your trading life either for better or worse. The simpler the process, the better results it will give. This is because you are dependent on your process to make money, and the more complex the process, the more time it will take to reach any decision within a particular time frame. The more time you take to make a decision, the worse the results become.

What do you mean by a breaker candle?

Any candle that breaks and closes above or below the previous candle's high or low is a breaker candle. The candle which breaks the high of the previous candle must be a bullish candle (green/blue) and the candle which breaks the low of the previous candle must be a bearish candle (Red).

Why are we more concerned with the breaker candle than any other candle?

Let's understand this with a simple example. If you are a fitness freak and attempt to lift a larger weight than your previous limit, but are unable to lift it, does it prove that you've grown up? Or if you actually lift a larger weight than your previous limit, will it be considered as progress?

The same thing happens in the stock market. The breaker candles show progress. In other words, breaker candles continue the trend.

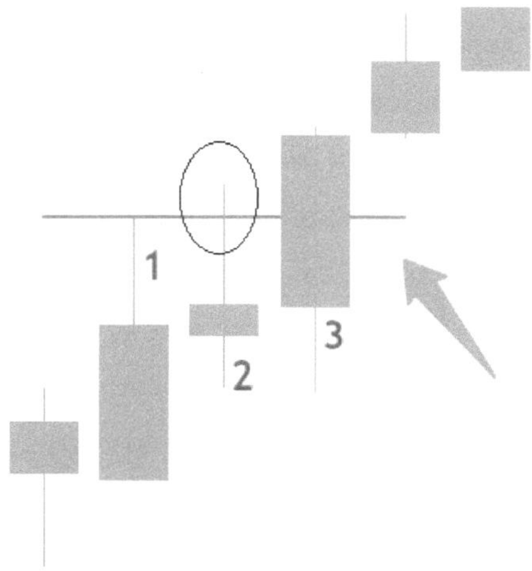

In the above chart, the first candle represents your previous highest limit, the second candle represents your failed attempt to break the previously set limit, and the third candle represents your progress. Doesn't it? We are more concerned about the progress, rather than the attempts. In the real stock market, we focus more on the breaker candle, because they represent the continuation of the trends. They represent strength. They represent progressive power.

The breaker candle in simple words is the candle which shows the progress of the trend. This signifies that there is still strength available to move forward. If you don't see any breaker candles in the trend, it signifies traps or false movements in any direction.

Any price action candle that is created (on any timeframe), represents the combined strength of bulls and bears. The maximum strength the bulls can exhibit is termed as the high of the candle, and the maximum strength the bears can exhibit represents the low of the candle. In every candle, by looking at the color, you can identify who is displaying more strength – the bulls or bears. Why do we get bullish and bearish candles all the time? It's because every moment someone is buying and someone is selling depending on their own analysis. Whoever puts in more strength moves the market in their direction.

For example, if a candle closes as red, it tells us that the bears are in power. Any candle that closes green represents the strength of the bulls. If any candle closes green, without any wick or shadows, it represents 100% strength of the bulls, with 0% interference from the bears. Where there is a red candle without a wick and shadow, it signifies 100% strength of the bears without any interference from the bulls. The color of the candle is derived from the strength put in by each team – the bulls and bears. The bulls and the bears determine the flow of the market, displaying their strength.

Types of Breaker Candles

In a broader sense, breaker candles can be classified into two categories:

- Absolute breaker candles
- Relative breaker candles

Absolute Breaker Candle

Any breaker candle that starts a new trend, whether it's the upside or downside, is called an ABC. Absolute breaker candles always occur near the peak or at the bottom of the previous trend.

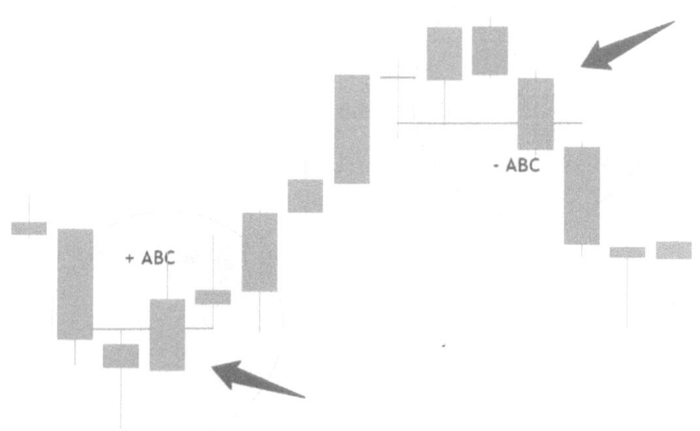

If you look at the above chart, the downtrend was interrupted by the positive ABC candle, breaking the high of the previous downtrend, which we refer to as the absolute breaker candle. It is an attempt to start a bullish trend. Absolute breaker candles attempt to reverse the trend. The negative ABC candle interrupted the upside trend, attempting to start a bearish trend.

Relative Breaker Candle

Any breaker candle that continues the existing trend is called a Relative Breaker Candle (RBC).

The low and high of every RBC comprise the trend validation points. This means that any candle breaking on either side of the previous RBC becomes the new relative breaker candle if it breaks in the same direction of the trend. If it breaks on the opposite side of the trend, it is an absolute breaker candle.

Breaker candles that occur after an ABC in the same direction are known as RBCs. You will see RBCs in the next two to four candles after an ABC appears, except in the case of Consolidation Phases or No Trade Zones.

With every RBC, we get a new trend validation point. With the help of a new RBC, we can continue the same trend. In fact, RBCs confirm the continuation of the trend. Until we get to the opposite side of the absolute breaker candle, we continue in the same trend with the trend validation points (the highs and lows of the RBCs). The RBC tells you when exactly the trend changes, allowing you to make your trading decision easily and effectively.

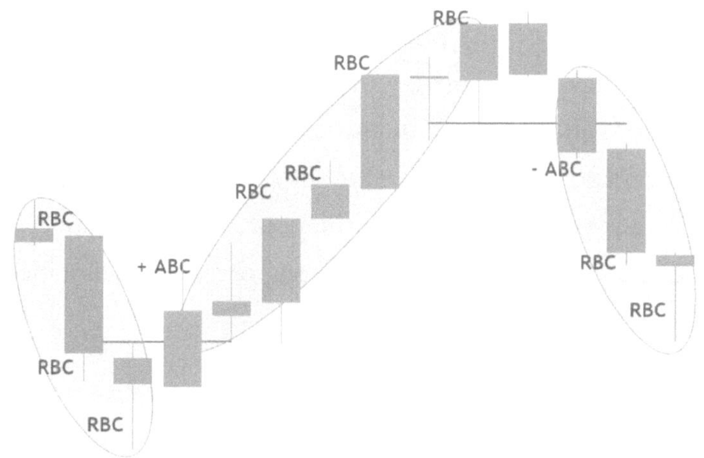

In the above chart, all the relative breaker candles are marked as RBCs. To start a trend, there must be an absolute breaker candle followed by a RBC. RBCs confirm the beginning of a new trend. With the help of trend validation points, we can identify whether a trend will continue or come to an end.

No Trade Zone

The price zone where the bulls and bears fight and try to take control of the market or stock or indices or any tradable instrument is called a no trading zone. It acts as a strong support and resistance zone.

Why is it called the No Trade Zone? In this zone, a tug of war happens between the bulls and the bears to take control of the price and one of them will be the winner, taking the market in its preferable direction. So, the zone itself has the interests of both parties at stake. Unless and until one side takes the market in its direction, it is not preferred to enter the zone. Once the zone is clear, we can align with the winning party to place trades accordingly.

The question is how can we identify these zones using the Breaker Candle Technique?

Have you ever wondered how the fair price of any market, stock, indices or any other tradable instrument is determined? We know that if the current price moves far up from its fair price, then the bears will try their best to bring it down as close as possible to its fair price. If the price is way below its fair price, the bulls will try their best to hike it up to its fair price.

But how is the fair price of any instrument determined? Who decides what the fair price is for any stock indices or any other instrument?

Is the fair price determined in the same way for both shorter and longer time frames? Or does the set of principles to determine the fair price change based on the time frame? Is the fair price a specific fixed price or is it dynamic, depending on the demand, supply, buying and selling pressures?

In the era of Algos, the fair price is dynamic in lower time frames. It changes over time based on the demand, supply, buying and selling pressures. However, the fair price is more constant for longer time frames as it takes into consideration the fundamental parts of any business.

Let me explain it to you with an example: A market maker offers 1000 shares at Rs 100 each and 1000 shares at Rs 99 each. Now let's say retail trader A purchased 300 shares at Rs 99 and retail trader B purchased 700 shares at Rs 99. Now the offer that was available by the market maker at Rs 99 has been filled and he has an open offer available at Rs 100. However, if the retail trader wants to sell them, the same market maker will try to buy them at a lower price, say for example, at Rs 98, rather than purchasing them at the same or higher price.

Now the bid is available at Rs 98 and the ask is available at Rs 100 by the market maker, which is a balancing act of the price discovery system. We call this the spread. Let's say retail traders A and B sold their shares at Rs 98. Immediately, the market maker will change his bid to Rs 97 and ask to Rs 99. This is how the market maker creates a balance between buyers and sellers.

The balance created between the buying pressure of the buyers and the selling pressure of the sellers is called Technical Fair Price.

The No Trade Zone is the fight zone between both the bulls and bears. Depending on the strength of each party, the price will dynamically either go up or move down. If the price level goes up from this level, then the bears will get active to bring the price down to the previous fair price and vice versa, unless the technical fair price shifts to any other level.

By using the No Trade Zone, you will easily identify the strong points of the market, stock indices or any other tradable instruments, the price points that will act as support or resistance, and the price levels that an instrument can easily move between.

In the above chart, you can see a +ABC overlap with a –ABC. We refer to this as the no trading zone, because both the bulls and the bears fight to take the price in their preferred direction. Once the price breaks out from this zone, it gives very good returns.

No trade zones can be of two types: A bullish no trade zone and a bearish no trade zone. Bullish no trade zones are those where we get the +ABC first then the –ABC. It represents a bull run if it breaks out for the upside. A bearish no trade zone is one which represents a bearish trend if it breaks out for the downside.

An important point to keep in mind is that during a consolidation phase or in a market that's not trending, if a bullish no trade zone breakout happens for the downside, it can become a trap for sellers, and if a bearish no trade zone gets broken for the upside, it can become a trap for buyers. However, if during a trending market, let's say in a bearish market, we get a breakout of a bullish no trade zone for the downside, the trend continues unless it breaks out the upside of the bullish no trade zone.

In the above chart, we see a bearish trend which continues and we get to a bullish no trade zone. Thus, we will continue the trade for the downside until the price moves up and closes above the bullish no trade zone.

The above chart is of a bullish no trade zone during the consolidation phase, in other words, during a no-trending market. As I mentioned previously, during a no-trending market, if there are any overlapping zones (no trade zones), any opposite side breakout such as a downside breakout of a bullish no trade zone or an upside breakout of a bearish no trade zone, can become a trap. In this chart, you can clearly see it happening. A bullish no trade zone breakout happens on the downward side, trapping the sellers and moving in its direction.

Rules and Exceptions to the Breaker Candle Technique

A trend starts when you get an absolute breaker candle followed by a RBC. The trend continues with the subsequent RBCs until you see the opposite absolute breaker candle. The high and low of every latest RBC is termed as the Trend Validation Point (TVP). TVPs are used to track trends and trailing stop losses, which eventually helps in maximizing profits and minimizing losses. For example, if there is a bullish RBC, mark the high of the candle as the TVP and any further candle that closes above the TVP will be assigned as the new RBC and so on.

Entry

Enter the trade at the closing of the RBC with a few exceptions like zone breakouts. In case of zone breakouts, don't wait for the RBC to form. Enter the trade immediately. Keep the stop loss below ABC in case of a bullish trade or above ABC in case of a bearish trade. With every new RBC, trail the stop loss and TVPs.

TVPs help us track the trend. If two to three new candles don't break the latest TVPs, cut your exposure. Because if the trend is strong enough, it won't spend two to three candles within the range. If the TVP doesn't break, it means the trend is getting weaker and you must lower your exposure. If the non-breaker candle is relatively small, then the trade can be extended to four to five candles.

Remember, if you exit a trade, no matter how fascinating a scenario it might create again, once you are out, you are out. However, let's say the latest TVP is broken. You can enter the trade with the same rules, but this time, enter with a lower exposure than your regular trades.

EXIT

Exit the trade if the price hits the stop loss point. Always keep in mind that a stop loss is honored on a price closing basis, not merely on a touching basis.

Exit the trade when the trade comes to an end, meaning when the opposite side absolute breaker candle appears on the screen.

Exit the trade when the price enters any previous no trade zones.

Exit the trade if any two new non-breaker candles are within a visually big-sized candle, because this can turn into pump-and-dump action. Alternatively, once you get confirmation of the pump and dump action, place opposite side trades, as per the rules concerning the trade of big candles.

Exceptions

For any unusually big candle, place the stop loss at 50% of the same candle. Don't set it at regular TVP points. Avoid entering the trade if on a particular day, your stop loss has been hit twice (outside of no trade zones).

Buy low sell high

How can you enter a trade confidently? Let's say you receive good technical signals, but how confident can you be of the trade? What can make you lose your confidence?

Remember, the market runs on the 80:20 rule. Eighty per cent of the time it creates traps. Only 20%

of the time it gives good returns. Because of your trapped trades, you may lose confidence regarding your signals and strategies. Let's say, for example, you received a buy signal. You entered the trade but you didn't get the expected return and the price moved down. Now you don't enter the downside, considering your previous trade, but this time the market makes a bigger move or vice versa. You were on the sell side but a bigger player trapped you and reversed the price. You refrained from entering the buy side fearing you may get trapped again. But this time, the market gives very good returns.

Is it possible to solve this dilemma using the Breaker Candle Technique without any indicator? The answer is a resounding yes! Why do I say without any indicator? Because indicators are built to indicate, not to help you identify bigger trends and traps. The indicator may not help you decide whether to take a big risk on any particular trade or not. The Breaker Candle Technique can solve this problem for you. You can confidently place your trades following this rule: Buy low and sell high.

It is obvious that a trader can make money only when he purchases at a low price and sells at a higher price. This rule applies to every trader including the big players.

If you don't plan your trades following this principle, you will make mistakes along the way. In simple words, you must follow this principle of buying low and selling high. However, most traders face problems because the selling price doesn't go up from the buying price. Using this simple principle, you can overcome the noise that big players create to trap you.

The stock market never goes up or down in a single line. It moves in a zig-zag pattern. It goes up and comes down a little. It goes even higher from the last high then again comes down a little bit. In the Breaker Candle Technique, we refer to these comebacks as pullbacks or cooling phases. These pullbacks and cooling phases are created by the big players to confuse the retail trader so that they won't understand the actual direction of the trade.

Let us look at an example: Suppose you get an absolute breaker candle for the bullish side (+ABC) on point X and you entered the trade after getting a relative breaker candle (+ RBC). As the trade continues, you book profits after getting the opposite side absolute breaker candle (-ABC). A regular trader will reverse his trade after getting a relative breaker candle for the downside (-RBC) without keeping in mind that the downside trade has no free-flying zone, because strong support is available at the latest ABC. What you must keep in mind here is that the instrument coming down doesn't signify a negative trend; it is just the cooling-off period or pullbacks that big players create to trap the retail trader.

Unless and until the price moves below the latest absolute breaker candle (+ABC in the above example), the trend is bullish. In any market, during bullish phases, it's not advisable to place a downside trade. What I mean by the market here is any stock, instrument, indices or other tradable instruments where we can apply the Breaker Candle Technique. Remember, this technique can't be applied on option charts, as options are highly volatile and bigger swings are possible, which is outside the scope of the Breaker Candle Technique.

Till now, we talked only about the pulls backs of trades. Now, let's understand the traps. As the market runs based on the concept of buy low and sell high, if you find a scenario where the latest buy zone (+ABC) is higher than the previous sell zone (-ABC) or the latest sell zone (-ABC) is lower than its previous buy zone (+ABC), then it's highly likely that you will be trapped as the market movement is not normal.

Handling Traps with BCT

A bullish trap occurs when a trader believes the market is trending upwards, but the price suddenly drops, while a bearish trap occurs when a trader believes the market is trending downwards, but the price suddenly rises. There are many ways a retail trader can get trapped in the stock market. Let me share with you how traps are created by big players by using gaps and big candles.

Gap Opening

When the price of any stock, instrument, indices or any other tradable instrument opens above or below the previous day's close with no trading activity in between, it is called gap opening. There are two types of gaps:

- Time frame based gap occurs when the opening price is higher or lower than the previous day's close but within the previous day's price range.
- Day based gap occurs when the opening price is outside of the previous day's range.

It is most common to find day based gaps which are explained by different individuals over different platforms. However, both types of gaps have their own relevance and can't be treated the same. In the Algos era, you also find time frame based gaps. However, here is the secret: Algos does not take into consideration timeframe based gaps. Simply put, Algos won't keep track of price action movements on the basis of time frames, like a 3:30 p.m. candle and a 9:15 a.m. candle. What they do take into consideration is continuous price movement rather than the close of the previous day and opening of the current day. Computers don't keep track of change in days. From 3:30 p.m. to 9:15 a.m. there is a time lapse which is significant if it's an open gap, which we consider to be a hidden candle because Algos calculations don't change with time lapse.

Thus, it is essential we handle the different types of gaps in different ways. That's why we have a different set of rules in the Breaker Candle Technique to handle time frame based gaps and day based gaps.

Time frame based gap

In time frame based gap, the hidden candle plays a vital role. What is the hidden candle? The candle between 3:30 p.m. and 9:15 a.m. is called the hidden candle. It is either categorized as ABC or RBC depending on its color. If it opens upside that means the hidden candle is green and vice versa.

There is a common saying in the industry that if a stock opens gap up, opt for a bearish trade and if it opens gap down, opt for a bullish trade. Logically, if this is the case, then why is there a need to open gap? Why is it necessary to create a hidden candle? Unless and until you know the no trade zones, from where the price can get reversed, it is foolish to trade adversely.

In the above chart, there is a gap up opening. This analysis is only for the gap scenario. Don't apply it to regular trades. Mark the high and low of the first candle and wait for the opposite color candle to appear.

In our chart the first candle is a bullish candle, so we will mark its high and low as a bullish reference zone for that particular date. This reference zone can't be carried forward to the next day. We wait for a bearish candle, which occurs in the third candle. We mark the high and low of the bearish candle as the bearish reference zone. This reference zone can't be carried forward to the next day. As soon as the breakout of any reference zone happens, assign the breaking candle as ABC (highlighted in the above chart).

Once you assign the reference zone breaking candle as ABC, wait for the RBC to confirm the trend. The RBC should appear immediately after the ABC. If the RBC does not appear in the next candle itself, then it's a weak case, so stay away from the trade. For example, if ABC appears and RBC appears immediately as in the chart above, then we enter the trade. If RBC doesn't appear immediately after ABC, it's better to stay away, because this price movement will eventually become a trap.

Importantly, the stop loss should be placed at the high of the bearish reference zone (if the bearish reference zone breakout happens) or at the low of the bullish reference zone (if the bullish reference zone breakout happens). However, if the reference zones are too big, it means you have placed your stop loss at a very far price. Alternatively, you can place your stop loss below the ABC (in case a bullish reference zone breakout happens) or at the high of the ABC (if a bearish reference zone breakout happens).

Day based gap

If there is a day-based gap, it means the current day opening price is outside of the previous day's price range. If this is the case, switch to opening range strategy rather than following the hidden candle strategy. Plot the Fibonacci on the opening five-minute range with the following levels: 0, 1, 1.382, 1.618, 2.618 and so on.

Plot the Fibonacci with the mentioned levels on both sides and wait for the price to break out of the gateway, that is between the 1.382 and 1.618 levels. If the market is not trending then it will move between the +1.382 and -1.382 levels. Once the price breaks outside of 1.618, it again continues the trend. The candle that breaks the gateway gets assigned as ABC and you place the trade without waiting for the RBC.

More importantly, the stop loss is placed at the 1.382 level. Your first target should be the 2.618 level, the second target the 3.618 level and the third target, the 4.618 level, with trailing stop loss to its prior target.

Let's get a clearer picture using the below chart:

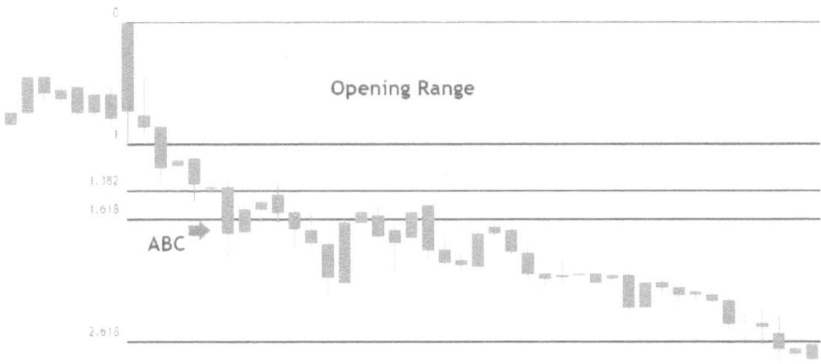

We have plotted the Fibonacci on the five-minute opening range, and marked the gateway levels, that is 1.382 – 1.618. and our target 2.618. As we get a breakout for the downside, we assigned it as the ABC and entered the trade keeping the stop loss at the 1.382 level. Any candle closing above the 1.382 level will hit the stop loss or we can book profit at our target set at 2.618.

Big Candles

You may have frequently seen in the market that a big candle forms and then eventually the price returns to its starting point with a few smaller candles.

Why do you think this happens?

When you see a big candle during trading hours, you may be confused about what to do next. Is this trend going to continue or should you book profit? You might consider entering the trade now, as the instrument shows strong movement. Or you might believe that since the price has moved so much, it's better to enter the opposite side trade. Thus, there are multiple convictions or 'biasness' on a particular move.

The market doesn't want the retail trader to make money. By market, I mean the big players. They don't want you to make a profit, so what they basically do is confuse the retail trader by creating a lot of noise.

Bigger players create noise by simply creating non-breaker candles here and there. But if this doesn't confuse the retail trader about the direction of the market, what they do basically is create too much noise by creating a big candle.

But why? Because it solves two problems for the bigger players.

Let's say, for example, the bigger players want to move the price upside, but there are so many retail traders who are in the same direction, so what do they do? They create a non-breaker candle here and there to confuse the direction of the instruments and limit the buyers. But let's say that even with this action, the traders don't move, assuming that the market can give them good returns.

This means they can handle this small noise or small losses.

As the retail traders don't move out of the trade, the big players will create bigger candles. In our example, they create a big bearish candle. Retail traders on the buy side will start exiting immediately, because they presume some significant event is going to happen, causing the price of the instrument to fall down. Through such kinds of big candles, big players solve two problems. One, they can limit the buyers (as per our example) and also trap other retail traders who have entered the trade on the downside, after seeing the big bearish candle.

How can you protect yourself from such noises?

You can filter out the small noise candles simply by defining the absolute breaker candle and RBC to the relevant candle.

In the Breaker Candle Technique, in the case of an unusually big candle (compare the size of the candle in reference to its previous 5 to 10 candles), expect a pump and dump action. This means the price will be pumped in a single candle or with multiple candles, and then gradually with small candles, the price will return to its starting point. Pump and dump actions have been banned. Big players are not allowed to use the pump and dump action, but as the price action looks like it, we refer to it as pump and dump in the Breaker Candle Technique. While identifying the visually unusual candle, should you consider the whole candle? No, the body size must be compared to the previous candles. Let's say, for example, a candle is formed with a bigger wick or shadow, but the body size is similar to its previous 5 to 10 candles, don't expect to see pump and dump action. Assume that it's a failed attempt to break out at a strong level.

How to handle big candles

How do you identify a big candle? Is there any mathematical formula or should you calculate any percentage? No, identify a visually big candle from where you started your analysis. Remember, not every big candle is met with a pump-and-dump action, because there might be some event or news that we are not aware of. So big candles can also mean the continuation of the trend rather than just noise.

There are certain rules I've put together to identify whether a big candle signifies the continuation of the trend or whether it will result in pump-and-dump action.

Let me simplify this for you with an example: Let's say there is a bullish trend going on (+RBCs continuing after +ABCs) and suddenly, we see a visually big candle.

This big candle can have two purposes. First, it can be a continuation of the trend, or it can be noise created by big players to trap retail traders. Instead of taking any immediate decisions on trade, wait for the opposite color candle to appear. (If the big candle is a bullish candle that is blue or green, wait for a red candle to form, or vice versa). Once you see the opposite color candle, mark the high and low of that candle as a reference zone, just like the gap open scenarios. Assign any candle that breaks the reference zone as a temporary ABC. If you get an RBC of the temporary ABC, (RBC must occur in continuation to the ABC) it is highly likely that pump and dump action will happen.

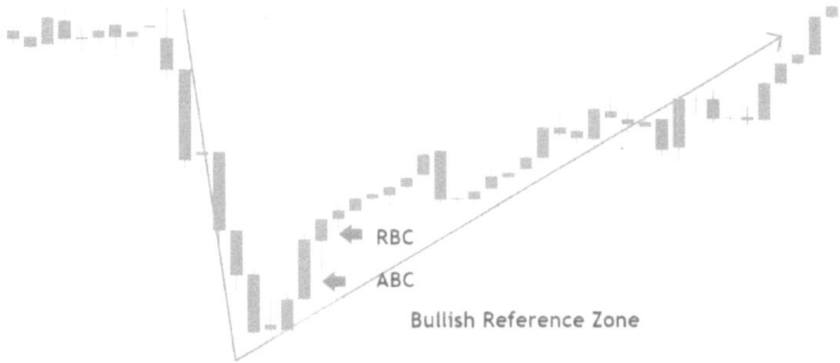

In the above chart, you can see an unusual price movement in six candles, a combination of ABC and RBCs. In such a scenario, wait for the opposite color candle and mark it's high and low as a reference zone. In our case, it is a green candle that is marked as a reference zone. Also, mark the latest candle of the unusual activity, so that you can identify whether the unusual candles will see pump and dump action or signify the continuation of the trend. In our example, the price broke the bullish reference zone which indicates pump and dump action. The candle that breaks the reference zone immediately gets assigned as ABC. Wait for the RBC to appear. Importantly, the RBC must be in continuation of the ABC or else it can become a trap just like I explained in gap trading.

Once you see the RBC in continuation of the ABC, enter the trade with the target till the start of the pump and dump action. Keep the stop loss below the bullish reference zone (or the high of the bearish reference zone in case of a bearish trend). When you combine the ABC and RBC, it must not be more than 50% of the price movement in this total pump and dump. For example, if the total pump and dump action is Rs 10 and the combination of ABC and RBC covers more than 50%, then your risk-to-reward ratio may cause problems.

Intraday and Continuous Trade

Trades can be classified into two categories. The first is intraday trading, where positions will not be carried forward to the next trading day, or overnight holding. The second is continuous trading, where you hold your trades for more than a day, for example, swing trades and short-term investment. For intraday purposes, the best time frame is five minutes. However, you can also trade on 15-minute time frames depending on the volatility. In continuous trading, we use a time frame of 15 minutes to one hour, as per the rules of the Breaker Candle Technique. There is a set of principles and conditions to be fulfilled before you decide to place any trade.

Intraday trading with BCT

How much will it help if you know whether the market is going to trend or not (consolidation)? Intraday trading using BCT is based on the ABC, RBC and no trading zone. Only with the help of these three parameters you will be able to identify where there is a trending market which will help you place a directional trade. If the market consolidates, you simply get out of the trade until the market transitions from the consolidation phase to the trending phase.

Previously, the opening range was considered to be the first 15 minutes of the day. However, in recent days in the Algos era, the opening range has shifted from 15 minutes to 5 minutes. We assign the first five-minute candle (opening range) of any day as the absolute breaker candle in intraday trading, depending on its color and position in reference to its previous day's opposite ABC. If the first 5-minute candle is blue/green, we refer to it as a +ABC and if it is red, we refer to it as –ABC. So, with the help of the previous day's opposite ABC, we identify whether the current day will be a trending day or become a trap for retail traders, depending on the buy low and sell high concept. Thus, if the first five minute candle of the day is –ABC, we look for the placement of the latest +ABC in the previous day and vice versa.

Secondly, check to see if there are any overlapping zones – the no trade zones. If there are any overlapping zones, then there is a high probability that any move in the direction of the subsequent ABC will become a trap and the trend will not be sustainable.

You should wait for the breakout of the no trade zone, in the direction of the former ABC. Usually, you will find that any trade placed in the direction of the prior ABC of the no trade zone always gives bigger and better returns. The candle that breaks the no trade zone (in the direction of the former ABC), will become the absolute breaker candle. Enter the trade immediately, after the formation of the ABC without confirmation of the RBC. Because any level breakouts and zone breakouts can only happen with strength. Thus, if you wait for the RBC, most often, it becomes too late to enter the trade.

Can you place a trade on the trap side? Yes, for sure, but it's important where you place your stop loss. If you get a break out in the direction of the subsequent ABC, you can enter the trade with stop loss below or above the candle that has broken the NTZ, depending on the direction of the trap. You already know that the trade is not going to last long, so it's not necessary to set the stop loss far away. However, if you get a breakout in the NTZ in the direction of the former ABC, place the stop loss at the opposite side of the zone rather than at the high or low of the ABC. Remember, the stop loss is hit only when the price closes below or above your stop loss line, depending on your direction of trade. Merely hitting the stop loss price and coming back doesn't mean that the stop loss has been hit.

Continuation/swing trades with BCT

Continuous trading begins with the rules of intraday where you enter with ABC followed by RBC. The only difference is that you carry forward the trades until you identify the reversal of the trend, that is the breakout of the opposite no trade zone.

As I already mentioned in the previous chapter, there are two types of no trade zones: The first is the bullish no trade zone, where the first ABC is green/blue and the subsequent ABC is red. The second is the bearish no trade zone, where the first ABC is red and the subsequent one is blue or green.

So, let's say you enter a trade after a bullish zone breakout for the upside. Hold the trade until the trend is over, that is, the breakout of the bearish no trade zone for the downside.

Things you need to keep in mind pertaining to continuous trade: When a trend begins, be it a bullish or bearish trend, you will get opposite side no trade zones. However, don't close your trade until the breakout of the opposite no trade zone.

If a no trade zone is formed when there's no trend, then any opposite side breakout can become a trap for the retail trader. However, let's say you've identified a bullish trend which is the breakout of a bullish no trade zone, and then a bearish no trade zone is on its way, until the trend is over. But since the current trend continues, there's no chance of a trap for opposite-side moves.

Simply put, any no trade zone followed by a breakout of a no trade zone can't be considered a trap until the subsequent no trade zone breakout for the opposite side occurs.

Your Takeaway

THE BOTTOM LINE

At some point, you must put the spreadsheet down and push the button. You know it's great to analyze things. It's great to complete the story. It's great to be a habitual learner and have a process that works. However, at some point, you must push the button. It's no use if you just sit there using demo accounts and think about where you might end up, without pushing the button. You must do it at some point. It's not always easy. But it's certainly easier if you have a process that works and a strong conviction, rather than just throwing darts in the dark.

Most importantly, avoid the behavioral traits that I mentioned are dangerous. If you see these traits in yourself eradicate them. There is no nice way to say it. Be adaptable, and be wary of the expert or the old hand. There are people who want to impart their wisdom to you, particularly if they are poor. Profitable traders focus on the future. Adaptable traders are open to change and to change their minds.

Accept that the hack doesn't exist. Pick up a pen and start writing things down. Think about your process. Think about what you want to achieve and think about how you want to achieve it. Is it harder than it used to be? I don't know. It has always been hard. Plenty of people trade and not all of them are geniuses. Like I said, it's not psychology. It's about gaining control of your beliefs and work ethic.

In conclusion, what does it take to be a successful trader? Awareness and attention to detail. If you don't have these tools, develop them. Curiosity is important too. You must be curious, otherwise, you wouldn't be reading this book. Street smarts and common sense come with time. Unfortunately, you will probably incur some losses as well. Nothing teaches us a good lesson like a good loss. That's life. The idea is to avoid noises and gain objectivity and emotional control. If you can do this, you will be in the game. Shut down your demo account. Seriously, stop wasting your time. You can't pay your bills with that. If you remain on your demo account for 12 months, you will end up with a grand total of zero real money.

We have had people come to our programs, spend time with us and then decide it's too hard. But they do push the button. They take a risk. If you take a calculated risk and do some work, you will get there. The people who don't get there are those who can't make up their minds. You must be honest with yourself and ask yourself the following questions: *Is this for me? Am I prepared to do the work to be profitable to pay my bills and turn it into something that's more than just a hobby?* I can't answer these questions for you. But, with any stock, at some point, you will have to decide whether you want to go long or short. If you really want it, and if you are going to do it, do it properly.

In the ideal world, we all get to a point where we are winning. The biggest fallacy is that when you make all this money, you believe you will live a great balanced life. Supercars, helicopters, big houses, I don't know what you are into. The point is, if you get to that point where you are winning, it is not the time to introduce some balance in your life. Having some balance in your life, developing a creative thought process and being interested in various things – these are the attributes that will allow you to get there. It took me a very long time to work this out for myself, trust me. This business shouldn't be all-consuming. If it is all-consuming, it is probably not going to work. To be honest, you probably have other things. It should be a means to an end, not the end in itself. It is very easy to be a slave to the market when in reality you know that the market should work for you. Remember, learning is a slow process, but once you master the skills, the J-curve of your life is really quick.

Now that you have finished reading this book, you are all set to start your journey. If you choose to give up now, it's not a big deal. But if you want to master your finances, better make up your mind.

"Do you think that the cost of financial education is high? Think of the cost of ignorance."

I leave you with this thought.

www.ingramcontent.com/pod-product-compliance
Lightning Source LLC
LaVergne TN
LVHW091102150826
845673LV00002B/695

9798890677525